THE SOKE OF PETERBOROUGH

A Portrait in Old Photographs and Picture Postcards

by

Judy Bunten and Rita McKenzie

S.B. Publications

To our families, especially our husbands Mack and Robert,
who have proved just how far a bottle of washing-up liquid can go!!

First published in 1991 by S.B. Publications.
Unit 2, The Old Station Yard, Pipe Gate, Market Drayton,
Shropshire, TF9 4HY

© Copyright Judy Bunten and Rita McKenzie 1991.

All rights reserved

ISBN 1.870708.81.4

Typeset, printed and bound by Manchester Free Press, Paragon Mill, Jersey Street,
Manchester, M4 6FP. Tel. 061-236 8822

CONTENTS

	Page		Page
Acknowledgements and Bibliography	iv	Ufford	49
Introduction	v	Marholm	50-51
The Soke of Peterborough	vi-vii	Etton	52
Map of The Soke of Peterborough	viii	Helpston	53-56
Market Square, Peterborough	1-2	Maxey	57-59
The Gaol House, Thorpe Road	3	Market Deeping	60-61
Thorpe Workhouse	4	Deeping St James	62-64
Thorpe Park	5	Northborough	65-66
Thorpe Hall	6	Glinton	67-69
Longthorpe	7-10	Peakirk	70-73
Orton Longueville	11-13	Newborough	74-77
Orton Waterville	14	Eye	78-79
Alwalton and Alwalton Lynch	15-18	Flag Fen	80
Milton Ferry	19-21	Woodston	81-82
Milton and Milton Hall	22-23	Fletton	83-85
Castor	24-27	Stanground	86
Water Newton	28-29	Peterborough Magistrates Court	87
Wansford Station and Wansford	30-36	Crown and County Court	88
Thornhaugh	37-38	Peterborough County Court	89
Wittering	39	Dogsthorpe	90-91
Burghley House and Stamford	40-42	Paston Valley	92
Wothorpe	43	Paston	93-95
Uffington	44	Gunthorpe	96-97
Barnack	45-46	Walton	98-101
Bainton	47	Werrington	102-104
Ufford and Bainton Home Guard	48	S.B. Publications	

Front cover: The Sheepwash, Fenbridge Road, Werrington, 1912

Title Page: The coat of arms of The Soke of Peterborough

ACKNOWLEDGEMENTS

The authors are indebted to the following people and organisations for their assistance:
Neil Mitchell for his great help with research.
Richard Hillier for his usual valuable assistance as Local Studies Librarian.
Mrs Shelton for loan of postcards, pages 46-49 and 59.
Mr Titman for loan of postcards on pages 67 and 68.
Mrs J. Harris for the loan of the postcard on page 57.
Nene Valley Railway for permission to use the postcards on pages 30 and 31
Douglas Thompson for permission to use the postcard on page 101.
Peterborough City Council, Museum and Art Gallery, for their permission to use the postcard on page 24.
Peter Harvey, Secretary of Peterborough Photographic Society, for the photograph on page 89.
Reg Wilcox, Minster Photographic, for photographs on pages 87 and 88.
Frank Rhodes of Lightwood for editing and proof-reading.
Steve Benz for publishing and marketing.
Numerous friends with valuable information.

BIBLIOGRAPHY

Boyden G., *The James Bradford Trust* a compendium
Bunch A. & Liquorice M., *Parish Churches In and Around Peterborough*
Cambs. Fed. of W.I.s, *The Cambridgeshire Village Book*
Day F.A., *The Deepings*
Earle D'A Willis F. MA, *The History of The Parish of Uffington With Casewick*
Mee A., *Northamptonshire*
Pevsner N., *Northamptonshire*
Willcock W.J., *Walks and Rides In and Around Peterborough*
Peterborough Advertiser, *Century Story 1854-1954*
Peterborough Advertiser, *Peterborough Story 1854-1979*
Peterborough Directories and Local Guide Books:
Leslie Webb, *Some Peterborough Buildings*, The Peterborough Society
Peterborough New Town, HMSO 1969

INTRODUCTION

Rita and I have collected postcards for many years and we have used some of our collection to take you on a tour of the Soke of Peterborough (the old Nassaburgh Double Hundred), bounded by the River Welland to the north, the River Nene to the south, and straying across the Old North Road to the limestone uplands on the west, and across to the vast flat plains of the Fens to the east.

Woven into the tour are the historical threads that bind us to the unique tradition of justice that is at the very roots of the existence of the Soke of Peterborough — so we visit The Guildhall on the Market Place, in whose Chamber met the Court of Quarter Sessions until the new Sessions House was built in 1840 on Thorpe Road: the Peterborough County Court in New Road built in 1873: the Magistrates Court in Bridge Street, opened in 1978: and the Crown Court & County Court in Bishop's Road, opened in 1987 — with the Cathedral reminding us of the Abbey's earlier powerful presence.

Heading westward along the valley of the Nene, with occasional detours across the boundary of the Nene to the villages on its south side, Orton Longueville, Orton Waterville and Alwalton, we turn north to Stamford and visit the home of Lord Burghley, Marquess of Exeter, whose forbears fought so hard to maintain the powers and privileges of the Soke of Peterborough.

Then along the Welland valley, with its pretty villages, eastward to Maxey, Peakirk and Glinton and on to Borough Fen, Newborough and Flag Fen.

South of Peterborough, the boundary of the Soke encompasses parts of Woodston and Fletton, with its neighbour Stanground just over the border; then back through the City Centre and northwards to the 'villages' of Dogsthorpe, Paston, Gunthorpe, Walton and Werrington, all of which have now been absorbed into the City of Peterborough, but whose roots stretch way back into the early days of the Nassaburgh Hundreds and beyond. Werrington has a special place with the choice of the cover photograph and finale of our tour. The village is very important to us — we both live there!

These postcards portray the photographic images of most of the villages within the Soke of Peterborough, but, far more than that, we hope that the wealth of history of this area flows through the script provided with each picture: the villages of local limestone and Collyweston slates with their ancient churches and houses: the rivers and their valleys: the grandeur of the Fens and the constant battle against flooding: the men and women who peopled the Nassaburgh Hundred and left us an ancient inheritance of administration that has withstood the test of time.

Most of all we trust your appetite is so whetted that you will set forth upon the open road and pay a visit to the villages of the Soke of Peterborough in the summer, and in the winter pay a visit to your local libraries, where there are wonderful books to tell you far more of its history than Rita and I can achieve in this little book.

Judy Bunten
Rita McKenzie
May 1991

THE SOKE OF PETERBOROUGH — ITS HISTORY

Mr W.T. Mellows, a well-regarded local historian, in his booklet on "The Local Government of Peterborough" said: "Of the various archaic titles of the administrative organizations of the estates of Peterborough Abbey, one has survived in the name of the modern county of the Soke of Peterborough, and the question is often asked by the man in the street 'What is the meaning of *The Soke*?' To give a simple and easily comprehensible answer to this question is a matter of some difficulty, and it will be necessary to begin with a general description of the earliest units of local government. The critical student will perhaps pardon some wide generalizations."

Several years have passed since those words were written and the Soke of Peterborough has become the victim of local government reorganisations so that Peterborough is now in the County of Cambridgeshire, and the Soke of Peterborough has faded into the mists of obscurity.

In the year 972 the Abbey of Peterborough was refounded by Bishop Aethelwold of Winchester, and endowed by King Edgar with (1) the grant of certain estates, known as the Eight Hundreds, and (2) a wide range of special privileges.

1) **The estates** — the Eight Hundreds — endowed to the Abbey of Peterborough comprised:
   a) Two Hundreds, or the Double Hundred of Nassaburgh, which later became the Soke of Peterborough. Nassaburgh, or the Nesse of Burgh (an earlier name for Peterborough) was the nose of land jutting out between the rivers Welland and Nene, from the limestone uplands in the West to the marshy Fenlands to the East.
   b) the remaining Six Hundreds lay in the Nene Valley between Oundle, Finedon and Kettering; a large proportion of Northamptonshire.

2) **The special privileges** granted to the Abbey of Peterborough were "freedom from the jurisdiction of king and bishop... (and sheriff)... (the freedoms being to hold the area) with SAKE and with SOKE, with TOLL and with TEAM and with INFANGENETHEF." these Anglo-Saxon words delineated the privileges granted to the Abbot to hold Manorial and Hundred Courts, to receive revenues and services from those Courts, to hold judicial courts with the power of punishing local offenders, and to try and hang thieves caught within the Eight Hundreds. The Abbot (who exercised these rights in the name of the Abbey) had all of these powers to the exclusion of the King himself and the Sheriff of Northampton — he ruled through his own officials at the Abbey. During the next 300 years the Abbot acquired additional rights — to use and maintain the Abbot's Prison (the undercroft alongside the Cathedral Gateway, now Smith Gore's offices), and to seize property from felons — the Abbey was vastly

enriched in medieval times by such ransoms. In 1329 the Abbot's rights were again expanded — he could hold prisoners until fines and dues were paid up and could execute judgement through his own Ministers (instead of Sheriff's Officers as elsewhere). In 1361 the Quarter and Petty Sessions were established — but PETERBOROUGH WAS UNIQUE IN THAT THE ABBOT CONTINUED TO RULE OVERALL. He set up Petty and Quarter Sessions, nominated justices and granted power to appoint, and that power continued right up to the Reformation.

"This right of judging in a private court and of taking the profits of jurisdiction was called SOC and SAC, and in course of time the area in which it was exercised was known as a Soke".

At the dissolution of the monasteries in 1539 these rights reverted to the Crown, but with the formation of the Bishopric of Peterborough in 1541 such rights were granted to the first Anglican Bishop of Peterborough, John Chambers but only over the Double Hundred of Nassaburgh, and were held until the third bishop, Bishop Scambler, surrendered these rights to his Sovereign Queen Elizabeth in 1576.

The Queen transferred the Lordship to William Cecil, Lord Burghley (later Marquess of Exeter), who thereupon became Lord Paramount of the Soke of Peterborough and Custos Rotulorum — keeper of the Rolls and Records, and hereditary Chairman of Quarter Sessions.

In 1888 the Local Government Act ensured that most local county administration was passed to County Councils. By the influence of the then Lord Paramount, the 3rd Marquess of Exeter, the Soke of Peterborough became an administrative County separate from "that of the residue of the County of Northampton", with its full powers retained, and successive Marquesses of Exeter fought for those rights to be retained — in accepting this the Lord Chancellor said: "... the Soke of Peterborough is unique".

The Soke thus survived as an independent administrative entity until 1964 when the Liberty of Peterborough Quarter Sessions was abolished and replaced by the County of Huntingdonshire & Peterborough Quarter Sessions, and in 1965 the Soke of Peterborough was forcibly wedded to the County of Huntingdonshire. In 1972 by the Local Government Act Huntingdonshire was absorbed into the new Greater County of Cambridgeshire.

We may have lost the Soke of Peterborough but Peterborough is still pioneering — we have the longest continuous records of justice being administered in the same place; a unique jurisdiction which tradition is continued today with our new County Court — a descendant of the original Abbot's Court of the Eight Hundreds — now a Combined Court Centre for civil and criminal cases.

THE SOKE OF PETERBOROUGH WAS UNIQUE

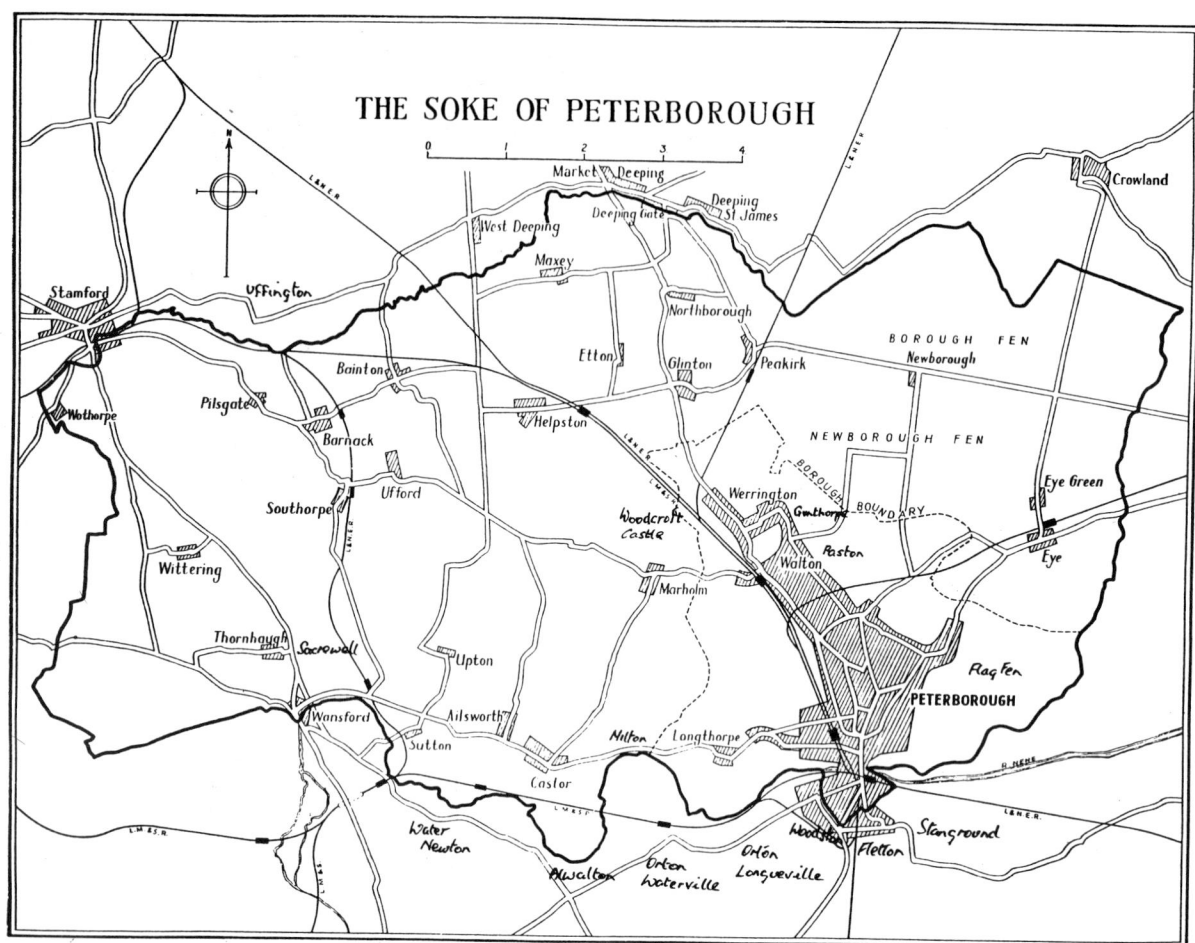

THE GUILDHALL, MARKET SQUARE, c. 1900

We start our journey around the Soke in the centre of the city at the Market Cross, which looks remarkably like the old Amsterdam Town Hall. Rebuilt or altered between 1669 and 1672 by John Lovin, the Corporation purchased the Market Cross for use as a Town Hall in 1874 and renamed it the Guildhall. The room on the first floor was used as a council chamber and at times when it was found to be too cold for meetings, the occupants moved over to the Talbot Inn; warming up in more ways than one! The council chamber was closed in 1933 when a new Town Hall was built in Bridge Street.

MARKET SQUARE, c. 1927

Looking between the pillars of the Market or Butter Cross towards the Cathedral, this was a typical scene. The old Market Square was renamed Cathedral Square in the early 1960s and originally covered a more extensive area than it does at present. The old records state that St John's Church, completed in 1407, was erected in the centre of the Market Place. In Oct 1963 the general market moved to its new position on the site of the old Cattle Market behind Broadway.

THE GAOL HOUSE, THORPE ROAD, c. 1910

The old Gaol House was designed in a castellated Norman-style and built in 1842 at a cost of £10,000. It was actually used as a prison for only 36 years. It continued in use as the headquarters of the Liberty of Peterborough Police Force and as the Liberty Magistrates Court, responsible for the Soke of Peterborough but excluding the City of Peterborough which had its own police force. The building has now been converted into a restaurant called the "Sessions House" and is overshadowed by the District Hospital.

THORPE WORKHOUSE, c. 1908

A new Union Workhouse was built in 1836-37 on Thorpe Road, west of Peterborough just past Aldermans Drive. Known as Thorpe Road House, the new building was let to Mr R. Noble at 2s 6d per head; Mr Noble being dubbed Master eventually. The Workhouse was built by John Thompson and Matthew Ruddle to hold 200 people, but by November 1855, it accommodated 80 men, 79 women and 140 children. Under the National Assistance Act 1946 the premises, now known as St John's Close, were vested in the Soke of Peterborough County Council. Standing in the foreground on the photograph are Mr and Mrs Webb, the caretakers at the time.

Entrance, Thorpe Park, Peterborough   55030

THORPE PARK

Looking towards Longthorpe, this view shows the Lodge House and one of the entrances to Thorpe Hall, prior to the construction of the roundabout at the end of Thorpe Road. A shepherd is seen driving his flock of sheep to market from Thorpe Park. Part of the shepherd's route would have taken him via Long Causeway to a slaughterhouse in Swan Place, now the site of a shopping arcade called Hereward Cross.

THORPE HALL, c. 1912

On 8 February 1653, John Ashley and Sampson Frisbey of Ketton contracted with Lord Chief Justice Oliver St John for thirty-eight windows of freestone from Ketton quarries, for a mansion at Hill Close, Longthorpe, which was later named Thorpe Hall. The postcard shows the eastern aspect with its splendid formal gardens. Materials taken from the old monastic buildings at Peterborough are said to have been used for other parts of its construction.

LONGTHORPE, c.1910

A charming village scene, looking down Thorpe Road towards Peterborough. In the distance the road curves left past a row of cottages by Longthorpe Green. In the garden of one of these cottages stood a very old stone cross-shaft some seven feet above the ground. Notice the group of children looking with curiosity at the photographer.

THORPE (LATER LONGTHORPE), c. 1906

A pond in the middle of Thorpe Road in Longthorpe village! Originally called Torpe, then Thorpe village, the Long prefix was added as the population of the village grew. The original hamlet of Thorpe was near Westwood, with the pond situated just near the entrance to Thorpe Tower. Notice the dog retrieving something for its master.

THORPE TOWER, LONGTHORPE, p.u. 1920

In 1263 the old Tower House, formerly known as West Hall, was built by Sir William de Thorpe, one of the knights of the Honour of Peterborough. The tower itself was probably added to the house at a later date. The building is a splendid example of a fortified Manor House. Until 1946, its early-fourteenth-century wall paintings were covered with whitewash. At the end of the second world war and after the Home Guard had finished with the building, traces of these wall painting's original colours were discovered on the walls.

LONGTHORPE, p.u. 1919

In this quiet backwater of Longthorpe village, the postcard shows a well-loved local character, Blind Billy Rollings, who lived in a small cottage opposite the Fox and Hounds Inn. He made his living as a chair and basket repairer, and was always to be seen tapping his way around the village, carrying a chair he had made or repaired. The old thatched Fox and Hounds Inn in the right background burnt down in 1928 and has since been rebuilt.

ORTON HALL, ORTON LONGUEVILLE, p.u. 1905

In the village of Orton Longueville, south of Longthorpe on the opposite side of the Nene Valley, stands this rather splendid building of Orton Hall. Of Tudor origin, the building was extensively altered and enlarged in the 1800s, and this West Front includes a conservatory built in the late Gothic style. Formerly the home of the Marquess of Huntley, then owned by the County Council and used as a school, it now awaits its next occupant. In its grounds stands a magnificent avenue of Wellingtonian pines, known as The Long Walk.

GORDON ARMS, ORTON, p.u. 1905

The tenth Marquess of Huntley was so struck by the design of the Queen Elizabeth in Sevenoaks, Kent that he decided to sketch it. This was later used as the basis of the design of the Gordon Arms which originally stood on a site near Orton Hall. In the early 1800s the old structure was moved further down the road nearer to Peterborough, on the opposite side of the Oundle Road, where it still stands. The well-dressed boys in the foreground are most likely waiting for the horse-bus to take them to school in Peterborough.

ORTON WAR MEMORIAL
ORTON LONGUEVILLE
p.u. 1920

The War Memorial is in the churchyard of Holy Trinity Church, Orton Longueville. The churchyard is surrounded by the trees of Orton Hall estate. The church was enlarged in 1675 with material from the church of All Saints, Botolphbridge (Bottlebridge) from a long-vanished hamlet which stood on a pilgrims' route leading to a ford on the River Nene opposite Longthorpe's Chapel of St Botolph.

ORTON WATERVILLE, c. 1919

A typically quiet village scene in Cherry Orton Road. On the left can be seen the Windmill public house which is still there today. The thatched cottage on the right now has a corrugated roof and is part of the garden of a modern bungalow built behind it. The name Waterville has nothing to do with the River Nene, which flows not far away, but is taken from the feudal family name of Waltreville.

ALWALTON, c. 1910

This postcard shows a view down the main village street to the church of St Andrew. Inside the church is a plaque to the memory of Frederick Henry Royce, born in this village on the 27 March 1863 — he later built the first Royce ten horse-power car in 1903-04 before becoming co-founder of Rolls-Royce. On the right is the tiny village post office and general store, recently damaged by fire, but still in business today. Maybe the cyclists, after posing for the photographer, intended to cycle down the village street to the River Nene and the lock gates for a lazy afternoon.

ALWALTON, c. 1910

The local hostelry, The Wheatsheaf Inn, is situated on what used to be the main A605 Oundle Road. Almost opposite was the blacksmith's forge which is now a private house. In St Andrew's churchyard are the resting places of Francis Arthur Perkins and his wife; the founder of Perkins Engines — world famous for their diesel engines. He lived in Alwalton Hall prior to his death on 15 October 1967.

ALWALTON LYNCH
p.u. 1909

This is another postcard taken from the "Stile" Series, published by B.B. of London. The lynch was a very popular beauty spot for courting couples — but did they really notice the scenery?

ALWALTON LYNCH, NEAR PETERBOROUGH.

ALWALTON LYNCH, c. 1909

The River Nene formed the southern boundary to the Soke of Peterborough, and flows on to Peterborough past Alwalton village. The word Linch means a ridge of land, boundary, or cliff. To the right of the river bank is a wooded river-cut cliff where Alwalton Marble was quarried. It was widely used in the East Midlands. There are carved effigies in Peterborough Cathedral sculpted from this marble and polished to a high sheen.

MILTON FERRY, late 1920s

From Alwalton Lynch a track led across the Nene Valley, crossing the railway line first and then crossing the river by this Ferry Bridge, the site of Gunwade Ferry. Built of stone, the bridge has three arches and includes two rooms on its north side; small craft can be stored there and launched via the steps. A tablet on the west side records that the bridge was built in 1716: ''at the sole cost and charge of the Right Honble. William Earl Fitzwilliam''. In the background Ferry House and Ferry Lodge (hidden behind the tree) flank the entrance to Milton Hall and Milton Park.

MILTON FERRY, 1906

The scene at the Fitzwilliam Hunt meet at Milton Ferry. At some distance to the east of Milton Hall were situated the kennels, built in 1767 in the form of a round medieval gatehouse. In the background can be seen Ferry House, named after Gunwade Ferry and formerly an inn. To the right is Ferry Lodge, now demolished and ready to be moved to a new site.

MILTON FERRY, c. 1910

A view of the A47 that will soon be just a memory! This gatekeeper's lodge, built in nineteenth-century decorative style and known as Ferry Lodge, stands by the main road to Peterborough, opposite Milton Ferry Bridge at one of the entrances to Milton Hall and Milton Park. It was once used by the Fitzwilliam family as a toll-house both for the road and bridge tolls. About a mile down this road, towards Peterborough, there is another entrance with Thorpe Lodge.

MILTON, c. 1915

Soldiers from possibly the East Anglian Divisional Engineers RE(TF) are shown crossing over a bridge on the lake at Milton. Their headquarters and both field companies were actually based in Bedford, but it is possible that Milton Park was a suitable place for an annual camp. Notice the temporary bridge made out of barrels, planks and ropes.

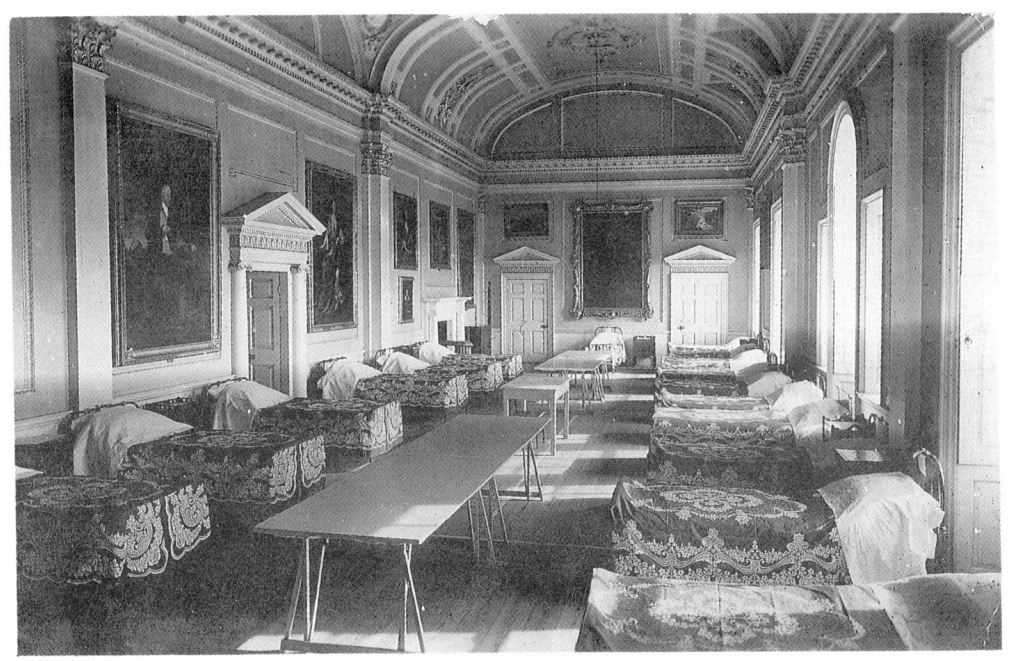

MILTON HALL, p.u. 1916

This postcard was sent by a patient convalescing at Milton Hall, when used as a Military Hospital in the first world war. The message reads, "This is the ward where we sleep. I am most comfortable here. From your old chum Bugler."

CASTOR, c. 1900

Photographed on the Peterborough Road, at the bottom of Loves Hill or Castor Hill as it is now called, a horse-bus is shown picking up passengers after its difficult descent down the steep hill into the village. On the right is the George and Dragon, a thatched inn built in 1703 and kept by Ann Upchurch at the turn of the century. The building is now a private home called "Dragon House".

CASTOR, c.1910

Dedicated to St Kyneburga, third of the four daughters of Peada, King of Mercia and founder of Peterborough Abbey, this church stands in absolute grandeur on high ground overlooking the lovely stone buildings of Castor village and the valley of the River Nene. This beautiful Norman church has the date of its consecration, 17 April 1124, recorded in relief on a semi-circular stone tablet built into the wall over the Priest's Door. ("The most important Norman Parish Church in the county" - Nikolaus Pevsner.)

CASTOR, p.u. 1944

From an early Peterborough Museum series of postcards, this postcard is entitled: HUNT CUP VASE. ROMAN. AD 135-200. CASTOR. Height 21.8 cms. Castor parish in Roman times adjoined the important settlement and army camp of Durobrivae, strategically aligned on both sides of the Nene and the important Roman Road of Ermine Street (A1). This Hunt Cup Vase is an example of "Castor Ware" - a thriving pottery industry in Castor and the Nene Valley area which existed in Roman times.

"THE FITZWILLIAM ARMS" NEAR PETERBOROUGH.

CASTOR, late 1930s

The Fitzwilliam Arms on the Peterborough Road presents a most attractive and inviting aspect to the weary traveller. All needs are provided for: a bus stop right outside the front door; a Power petrol pump; Allsopp Draught Ale on tap; deckchairs at the ready with shade provided; and parking spaces neatly marked — and vacant! What more could a customer want?

Water Newton Mill Head

WATER NEWTON, p.u. 1909

This small village stands on the south bank of the River Nene and was originally a Roman settlement called Durobrivae (the fort at the ford). In the Domesday survey three watermills are mentioned at Water Newton. The present mill, which replaced an older structure, has a date of 1791 and has now been developed into five quality dwellings; far different from the words of the poem on the next page.

THE MILL, WATER NEWTON.

WATER NEWTON, p.u. 1909

An excerpt taken from a poem entitled 'Newton Mill' published in 1928 described how the front of the mill must have looked in those days:

No sound of wheel
Turning with flash of spray comes from the mill,
Its voice of toiling now is hushed and still.
The window panes
Are broken, and the oaken doors
Stand open to the rains,
And moss grows green upon the rotting floors.

WANSFORD STATION - EARLY 1900'S

WANSFORD STATION, NR STIBBINGTON, early 1900s

Located close to the A1 near Stibbington, Wansford Station was designed in an impressive Jacobean style by William Livock, reflecting its importance as a road-rail transfer point. The centre door led to the booking office and platform, and the door on the left to the Station Master's house. After the station was closed by British Rail, the building was taken over by the Peterborough Railway Society in the mid-1970s, and is now occupied by the Nene Valley Railway.

WANSFORD STATION, c. 1910

Constructed in 1845, this was the first railway line to reach Peterborough. The line ran from Blisworth on the main line between London and Birmingham, via Northampton, Thrapston, Oundle and Wansford to Peterborough. The level-crossing and signal-box stand in the right background beyond the main station building.

WANSFORD, c. 1912

This street scene in Elton Road shows the Haycock Hotel and Wansford Bridge in the background. On the right can be seen the Methodist Chapel which opened on 11 October 1900. A new bypass and bridge over the River Nene, carrying the Great North Road opened 22 March 1929. This scheme preserved the historic Wansford Bridge which carried the former main road.

Peterborough (0733) 555222

Memory teaser

Schooldays recalled

THE winner of this week's Memory Teaser is Mrs P. Wilkinson of Western Avenue who correctly idenified the picture as of the ld Fletton School. Mrs Wilkinson was only one f her family who atended this school; her ather and his family and er sister were all eduated there. She left just s the war started.

Other correct entries inluded Mr Baxter from endrick Close, Stanround, who recalls that he school stood near the ailway bridge in High treet, although High treet was called Love Lane when the school was built. He started there in 1936 when Miss Berridge was headmistress.

Mrs W. Noble remembers many other teachers, including Miss Moore, Miss Williams, Miss Wilson and Mr Alcock, the local astronomer. She also mentions that in 1939-40 local children lost some education because the evacuees used the school on Tuesday, Thursday and Saturday, leaving Monday, Wednesday and Friday for local children.

Mr R. Clifton was in the headmistress's class in the 1930s and writes that all the children were on their best behaviour because she used to put the tip of the cane in the classroom's open fire until it glowed. The sight seemed to be enough because Mr Clifton says the cane was never used.

To win £5 in this week's competition, send your entries to Memory Teaser, The Citizen, 57 Priestgate, Peterborough, PE1 1JW.

Photograph courtesy of Rita McKenzie.

WHAT'S ON: *Entertainment listings in The Eveni*

A haven from the c

AROUND 150 people are thought to be sleeping rough on the streets of Peterborough every night.

Being homeless with nowhere to go is barely tolerable in the summertime – but during the cold winter months, with no protection from sub-zero temperatures, sleeping rough can sometimes lead to tragedy.

Bosses at the Haven night shelter in Cromwell Road, Peterborough, appealed through The Citizen

***KIND-HEARTED** readers have rallied to help the Haven night shelter's blankets appeal for city homeless – more than 1,000 blankets have been donated so far.*
The Haven has just 12 beds to offer overnight accommodation and is usually full, but those who cannot be given shelter are usually provided with a warm blanket to keep out the freezing winter temperatures.
Today Jean Lowndes looks at the work of the Haven which is open every day of the year.

to cope with Peterborough's growing homelessness problem.

Those turned away look for shelter in derelict houses, garages or under railway tunnels.

Steve said the Haven was overwhelmed by the tremendous response to the blankets appeal and he wanted to thank everyone who had donated.

"We are always grateful for donations of

WANSFORD, late 1930s

The Haycock Hotel stands on the south side of the River Nene, just over the border with the Soke of Peterborough. This fine old inn has the date 1632 on a stone (possibly added when rebuilt), and was one of the most important inns where the stage coaches stopped their four-day journeys along the Great North Road from London to York. The hanging sign and the painting over the door depict the legend of the Inn's name, which is based on a story dating from the seventeenth century and told in a doggerel rhyme by Richard Braithwaite.

"The Haycock," Wansford-in-England.

WANSFORD

Barnaby on his haycock — topiary style! The legend in rhyme is included in "Drunken Barnaby's Four Journeys to the North of England" - a scarce little book first published in 1638 by Richard Braithwaite (1588-1673). Barnaby visited Wansford on his third journey, when the plague was prevalent in the village. The usual inscription "Lord have mercy on me" over a plague-stricken dwelling drove Barnaby out of the village to the riverside, where he fell asleep on a haycock (pile of hay) with the result recorded below:

"On a haycock sleeping soundly
The river rose and took me roundly
Down the current: people cry'd,
Sleeping down the stream I hy'd:
"Where away", quoth they; "From Greenland?"
"No, from Wansforth-brigs in England".

WANSFORD, 1914-1918

Troops marching across the old bridge over the River Nene with the ancient church in the distance to the north; maybe the soldiers were on their way down the Great North Road to Wansford village and Station further south. The old bridge, only 14 feet wide at some points, has thirteen arches, and at its narrowest part there are twelve v-shaped refuges for pedestrians. In 1795, part of its southern side was rebuilt after considerable flood damage.

WANSFORD, p.u. 1926

The old Mermaid Inn stood on the North Road in Wansford. In 1937 the council purchased the Mermaid in order to carry out a major road improvement and diversion. The inn was demolished, road works put into effect and the diversion opened to traffic in June 1941. The outbreak of war halted the scheme and it was not completed until November 1946.

THORNHAUGH, c. 1960

Sacrewell Mill, on the east side of the A1, was rebuilt in 1755, probably on a site mentioned in the Domesday Book. It ceased its working life in June 1965 and has now been converted into the Museum of English Rural Life, run by David Powell who has known Sacrewell since childhood and lived there for 40 years. A magnificent wisteria covers the front of the Mill House; with the Mill roof standing high in the centre. The Mill Pond is to the left of these buildings. Sacrewell is named after a sacred well in Sacrewell Field, near Sacrewell Lodge, Thornhaugh; a settlement having been on this site since prehistoric times. Sacrewell Farm, of 575 acres, is a working farm administered by the William Scott Abbott Trust; a charitable trust devoted to agricultural improvement, education and research, and administered by the Royal Agricultural Society of England. Sacrewell Farm and Country Centre, welcomes hundreds of visitors with open arms as evidenced by its motto: ''Down the Hill to see the Mill, We are always Open''.

THORNHAUGH, p.u. 1915

The Lodge (now known as Oaks Cottage) and the grand ornamental wrought-iron gates at the entrance to Thornhaugh Hall were built in 1913-14 for Stanley Brotherhood by John Cracknell of Peterborough, with stone excavated from the quarries in Bedford Purlieus. Stone was also quarried near the Hall and the empty pit converted into a rock garden afterwards. The Hall was destroyed by fire on 24 November 1937, but was fully restored. In the book *Backstairs Life in a Country House* by Eileen Balderson, the author remembers: "From my bedroom at Thornhaugh I could see the grounds... it really was a picture postcard view, and on a fine warm night I loved to sit at my window to enjoy the vista of fountains and woods dripping with moonlight. It would have made a lovely setting for a romantic film."

DE HAVILLAND 9A

WITTERING, 1916-1919

"Home of the Harrier" is how Royal Air Force Wittering is proudly described today. In its early operational days, it was home to the De Havilland 9A biplanes which were based at Wittering in 1916-1919 and flew from Numbers 1 and 5 Training Depots. Throughout the Battle of Britain, detachments of the Wittering Squadron were involved, flying from forward bases at Northolt, Eastchurch and Biggin Hill.

BURGHLEY HOUSE, STAMFORD c. 1910

These neo-Jacobean west gates known as "Bottle Lodges" were built by the old Great North Road on the way into Stamford from Wansford. Designed by Legg in 1801 they show the English fondness for harking back into history. They are truly a grand affair with ogee-shaped turrets and three archways surmounted by the coat of arms of the Marquess of Exeter.

BURGHLEY HOUSE, STAMFORD, c. 1915

This is one of the largest of the Elizabethan mansions constructed mostly of Barnack stone, from the designs of John Thorpe, and built for William Cecil, the first Lord Burghley, (1520-1598) Lord High Treasurer to Queen Elizabeth I. His descendants were created Earls of Exeter in 1605 and Marquesses in 1801. The house has 145 rooms built around a courtyard and is surrounded by Burghley park, its boundaries extending seven miles, situated in Stamford Baron on the outskirts of Stamford, but within the Soke of Peterborough.

Stamford.   St. Martins Church, The Gt. North Road.

STAMFORD, p.u. 1905

High Street, St Martins, where the boundary of the Soke of Peterborough divides Stamford from Stamford St Martins (Stamford Baron). This splendid street, bounded by seventeenth-century Georgian stone houses, was the route of the Great North Road into Stamford. At the foot of the hill, on the left, the George Hotel still has rooms inside labelled ''London'' and ''York''; waiting rooms used in the days of the stagecoach. St Martins Church contains the tomb of the first Lord Burghley, and in its churchyard is buried Daniel Lambert (1770-1809), ''the fattest man who ever lived in England'' — 52 st 11 lb at the time of his death.

WOTHORPE, p.u. 1906

A clear view of the ivied ruin of Wothorpe Towers, photographed from the old Stamford Road, now bypassed by the A43, which climbs up to Easton-on-the-Hill. The ruin is all that remains of a house built in 1600 by Thomas Burghley, first Earl of Exeter, so that he "could escape from Burghley House at spring-cleaning time". It stands on the site of an ancient nunnery which was linked with Crowland Abbey. In 1758 much of its stone was taken to build the stables at Burghley House. Wothorpe Towers are in the Soke of Peterborough but nearby Wothorpe Drift is in Lincolnshire.

UFFINGTON, c. 1905

Right on the north-western boundary of the Soke is the village of Uffington. In 1673, the Hon. Charles Bertie bought the Uffington Estate and built Uffington House, completed c. 1687. It was recorded in 1678 that he paid £200 for lead and £5 8s 0d for 18,000 nails. On 19 December 1904, fire broke out in a room at the top of the house and quickly spread through the building. The majority of the contents were destroyed with the exception of the furniture, pictures and books on the ground floor.

BARNACK, 1915

Barnack Church, built of stone from the large local quarry, retains spectacular work dating from the Saxon era. The tower and spire were constructed in four stages, of which the lower two are entirely Saxon work dating from c. AD 1000. The belfry and spire were added about 200 years later. In the north aisle, there is a perfectly preserved tenth-century Anglo-Saxon sculpture of Christ in Majesty, and a fine thirteenth-century font. The church is well worth a visit and is one of the architectural treasures within the Soke of Peterborough.

45

BARNACK POST OFFICE.

BARNACK, c. 1920

Published by Charles H. Whittingdon, proprietor of The Stores in Barnack, with probably one of his staff standing in the shop's doorway. In the village churchyard is the tomb of George Gascoigne (born 1525), one of the founders of English Literature and a great adventurer. Charles Kingsley, author of *Westward Ho!*, lived in Barnack for 7 years of his childhood at his father's rectory; now known as Kingsley House.

BAINTON, c. 1912

This tranquil village scene, with St Mary's Church featuring prominently, has altered slightly since this picture was taken, modern bungalows having been built to the left and right. The bicycle leaning against the gate is reputed to have belonged to a local butcher who used to ride to his field to select and slaughter livestock for his shop!

UFFORD AND BAINTON HOME GUARD, 1941

In early 1940, and with the threat of invasion by Germany very apparent, the Government reinforced the nation's defences by forming the Home Guard. There were no shortages of volunteers and villages around Peterborough were no exception. The above photograph shows eleven men of the Ufford and Bainton Home Guard.

Left to right: Bert Saunders, "Grainey", Les Bradley, Roger Enderby, unknown, Ted Tomblin, Bloodworth, G. Dunford, Ernie Jarvis, Chris Reedman and George Shelton (Commanding Officer).

UFFORD, c. 1914

Ufford Hall, built in the eighteenth century and home of Lord Airedale, is on the site of the former Manor House of Uphall. The village was also the home of the Torpel family. The photograph shows villagers watching the gathering of the local hunt. Can readers name any of the villagers on the right of the photograph? The former stable block and coach house of Ufford Hall are now attractive residential homes called Fountain Court.

MARHOLM, p.u. 1915

Amongst the stately cedar trees, on the west side of the road between Marholm and Castor, lies St Mary's Church, built in the twelfth century and formerly dedicated to St Guthlac of Crowland. The church is the burial place of the Fitzwilliam family who have been in residence at Milton Hall since 1502; there are several imposing monuments to members of the family inside the church. Sir Christopher Wren married his second wife, Jane Fitzwilliam, here in 1676.

MARHOLM

The Fitzwilliam Arms with the inn sign depicting the family crest and Latin motto: "Appetitus Ratione Pareat" meaning "May your appetite obey reason" or "May your desires be reasoned". The topiary hedge was planted by a former landlord, Mr Fanthorpe, and is said to represent Earl Fitzwilliam, wearing a top hat and holding a tankard in one of his hands. This hedge is over one hundred years old, albeit sadly vandalised in recent years. However its presence there over the years has caused the locals to rename this hostelry The Green Man.

ETTON, 1892

This Bastion Tower is part of the fortified Manor House of Woodcroft. Built in c. 1280, it stands in a lonely position within the parish of Etton. During the Civil War, it became a Royalist stronghold. The Royalist, Dr Michael Hudson, was besieged in the tower on the 6 June 1648 by Parliamentary forces. Trying to escape, he hung from the battlements by his finger tips, but a Roundhead soldier cut his hands off at the wrists and he dropped into the moat where he was hunted down and killed. The character of Dr Rochecliffe in Sir Walter Scott's novel *Woodstock* was based on the experiences of Dr Hudson.

HELPSTON, c. 1920

Seven miles north-west of Peterborough lies the village of Helpston, with its attractive buildings built of limestone and Collyweston slates from the local quarries at Barnack and Collyweston. At the crossroads, in the heart of the village, stands the fourteenth-century village cross. Over the centuries local people gathered here for markets and important village events. The cross has a heart-shaped base and it is said that local people swore by the Heart of the Cross, a symbol of the Holy Heart of Jesus, to emphasise the value of their bargains. Shown on the left is the pillar memorial erected in 1869 to John Clare's memory, with quotations from his poems on the sides of the monument. In the background and behind the trees is St Botolph's church tower. In the churchyard and south-east of the porch, lies the simple tomb of John Clare with the inscription ''Sacred to the memory of John Clare, the Northamptonshire Peasant Poet. Born July 13, 1793. Died May 20, 1864. A Poet is born, not made.''

HELPSTON, 26 May 1921

The cottage in which John Clare was born, on 13 July 1793, was one of a group on the Castor Road, just past The Bluebell Inn in Woodgate. It was two houses when the poet was born, but was converted to three. When he married he took the house next door. The third doorway has since been bricked up again, whitewashed and a commemoration tablet placed where it was sited. On the back of this postcard is written: "The Peterborough Natural His. Soc. at Helpstone for the unveiling of the commemoration tablet on the cottage in which John Clare was born. Address by Edmund Blunden Esq. (Editor of *The Life of the Poet*)." They are grouped on the steps of the village Market Cross (see page 53) for this photograph. The Society's full name was Peterborough Natural History, Scientific and Archaeological Society. In 1924, its 52nd anniversary, membership reached over 1000 and its museum was in Park Road (the old Rink) — now Sheltons Store. This Museum housed a "conspicuous collection of John Clare's manuscripts and water-colour drawings and illustrations of the same by Montague Jones".

HELPSTON, c. 1908

Born at the Bluebell Inn, James Bradford JP endowed these six almshouses standing near the crossroads at Helpston. They were built at a cost of £4000 by a local builder, Mr Daniel Crowson, and the first six residents moved in in May 1908. The Lord of the Manor, G.C.W. Fitzwilliam, was so touched by Mr Bradford's generosity that he donated the land for the building.

8 Maxey Road, Helpston

HELPSTON, c. 1940s

Here the road from Maxey leads into Helpston, birthplace of the peasant poet John Clare. Some of John's poems, descriptive of the birds and flowers, the sights and sounds of the countryside rank high in English rural poetry. On the left, in place of the old cottages and pump, now stand modern dwellings, with the wall of the cemetery visible on the right.

MAXEY, c. 1926

The name Maxey is derived from Maccus' Eige or the island of Maccus, inhabited between AD 650 and AD 850. Excavations in the river gravels of the Welland have revealed evidence of widespread prehistoric settlement, with Danish influence. This view of High Street, looking east, was taken in more recent times! The Blue Bell public house dominates the scene with its hanging sign depicting on one side a blue bell of the ringing variety and, on the other side, a bluebell of the woodland flower variety. On the right, next to The Blue Bell, is the village shop — since 1989 a private dwelling at no. 41 with "Circa 1600 Woodyers Ferthing" on the lintels. The Morris Cowley standing outside the village shop and post office was owned by Roland, son of Mr and Mrs Frank Frost, the owners of the shop. From a container on its dickie seat, Roland sold ice-cream around Maxey village. On the left is Sunrise Cottage.

MAXEY, 1909

From a Minute Book dating from 1855: "On Sunday June 20 1909 special sermons were preached morning and evening by Rev. W.S.T. Merson of Grantham and on the following day, Monday 21st June, Sir Joseph Crompton-Rickett M.P. (whose father was born at Lolham Mill, Maxey) preached to a large congregation (in the afternoon) which filled the church to overflowing. A Tea followed in the Council Schoolroom when the large company present were accommodated at three sittings. In the evening an open air meeting was held in front of the Church presided over by Sir Joseph Crompton-Rickett M.P." Mr Reginald Coleman was the Minister in 1909. Over the door is written "Erected AD 1809 Rebuilt AD 1862". In 1978 the Church, which stands in West End Road, became the United Reform Church. The old cottage next door has disappeared and in its place is a modern house.

MAXEY, 1919

This interesting photo from the sporting history of Maxey was taken for the 1919-1920 season. Can anyone identify the missing names from this football team?

Back Row, L to R: unknown, Buster Pears, Harold Percival, unknown, unknown, Claude Harrison

Middle Row, L to R: Charles Bloodworth, Charlie Pollard, Ernie Wright

Front Row, L to R: Bert Hill, Reg Perkins, unknown, Sid Garford, Wilfred Pateman

59

MARKET DEEPING, c. 1910

"There's something so refreshing to behold
A broad and winding river whirl away".

The Welland by John Clare.

A lovely view of the River Welland from the bridge on the A15 Lincoln Road at Market Deeping. The river forms the boundary between the Counties of Lincolnshire and The Soke of Peterborough, Northamptonshire (now Cambridgeshire). By July 1842 this new stone bridge was finished and the "Lincoln Royal Mail" was the first vehicle to cross. It was built mainly of Portland stone and finished with red bricks from old cottages in Middle Row, Market Place, Market Deeping. Wharves and jetties led to the river, once serving corn merchants, granaries, mills and a distillery.

Church Street, Market Deeping.

MARKET DEEPING, p.u. 1905

A quiet day in Church Street, which leads to Halfleet and Towngate, and on to Bourne, 7½ miles further on the A15. On the left is Elm House, where Richard Todd lived for a short time. The larger houses beyond the gentleman in the cart have wall tablets "Erected by the Feoffees of Market Deeping Charity Estates AD 1819 and 1821". In the right foreground are the premises of Mr Henry Strickson, harness maker. Past the large gates stands the White Horse Hotel, famous for the 1920s dances in its Assembly Rooms. Against the background of trees stands Vine House — now demolished and replaced by Orchard Road and modern properties. In the far distance is the Church of St Guthlac, the saint who, it is believed, journeyed by road from Repton to what became Deeping St Guthlac, now Market Deeping, and on by river to a remote island in the fens, Crowland, in AD 699.

DEEPING ST JAMES, 1920s

At the junction of Church Street and Eastgate stands the Old Cross, built in the fifteenth century of Barnack rag stone and converted to the village lock-up in 1819 by Tailby Johnson, a local man. Above the shield is carved "Rebuilt AD 1819". On the left wall of the Cross, facing the Cross School (now the HQ for the local youth club), stands the village pump. This no longer exists, but its position is marked by the posts which stood in front of it. Behind the door, whose bolt and hinges remain intact today, and built within the Cross, is a small chamber containing three semi-circular stone seats, with attached chains, within the walls. The lamp on top of the Cross would have afforded very little light, and the cold clammy confines of this village lock-up must surely have dampened somewhat the spirits of its occupants.

LOW LOCKS, DEEPING. ST. JAMES.

DEEPING ST JAMES, early 1900s

Now electrically operated, Low Locks were last manually operated in the early 1900s, when the barges went from Spalding to Stamford. The first footbridge, built in the 1930s, had steel rollers underneath it which were used to help rowing boats across the wash stones. There is now a concrete bridge across the River Welland at this point. At High Locks (Deeping Gate) in 1676, Daniel Wigmore the Miller was prosecuted for causing a danger to the public by forcing the water by his locks, through the street, causing the formation of a pit in which two children were drowned.

DEEPING ST JAMES, c. 1912

The River Welland flows on from Market Deeping, past the High Locks, to this bridge, with Deeping St James on the left in Lincolnshire and Deeping Gate, in the Soke of Peterborough, on the right. The bridge, of three arches, and with two v-shaped niches on each side for pedestrians, was built in 1651, as indicated on the stone on the left-hand side of the right arch. On the other side of this same arch is a plaque saying, "In 1989 Peterborough District Best Kept Village. Proby Trophy." The man in the boat is Mr Holden, who worked for the River Authority; beyond the bridge are the Low Locks. On the left, at Bridge Foot, is The Bell Hotel (now the Mayfair). Next door is the draper's shop owned by Mr L. Shillaker.

NORTHBOROUGH, c. 1892

Cromwell's widow came here after the Restoration to spend the last years of her life with her son-in-law, John Claypole, Lord of the Manor. Situated on the A15 the ancient Manor House or "Castle" of the Claypoles was built about 1340 by Geoffrey de la Mare. Here we see Edith Nicholls and her small sister Florrie, whose family had tenanted the "Castle" under the Milton Fitzwilliams for at least four generations.

NORTHBOROUGH

Two famous widows lie here in the graveyard of St Andrews towerless church. John Clare's widow, Martha Turner, was moved to her last resting place from the cottage she occupied in the village. Also buried here, on 19 November 1665, the year of the great plague, are Mrs Oliver Cromwell and two of her grandchildren, Martha and Cromwell Claypole. In his will Cromwell Claypole asked to be buried "as near my grandmother Cromwell as convenience will permit".

GLINTON, c. 1912

The last days of August 1912 were described by a local newspaper as "this black week of rain and ruin". This scene shows the A15 Lincoln Road between Glinton and Northborough at Nine Bridges, where flood water was at least two feet deep. Although the floods subsided after a few days, thousands of acres of crops had been ruined. In some areas hay was so hopelessly soaked that farmers just ploughed it back into the ground.

GLINTON, c. 1920

When John Clare, the poet, took his early lessons with the schoolmaster Seaton in Glinton Church vestry, he would have seen this wonderful view of the lovely slender fifteenth-century needle spire on Glinton church from the Helpston Road, at the crossroads with Lincoln Road (A15) and High Street, Glinton. In later years he met Mary Joyce, his first love, here. On the left, on the corner of High Street, is the village store and post office. Proprietors of the Store and Post Office were Geo. Jones (1911), M Hayward (1927) and later Mrs Quincey and Miss Jones. Beyond these first buildings, Jessamine House remains today as the first house in High Street, with Garrick House next door. In the foreground, on the right, is the Congregational church and beyond that the Six Bells public house.

GLINTON, 1920s

Mr J. W. Levack, schoolmaster of Glinton Church of England School, School Lane, poses with some of his pupils.

Front row (left to right): Geo. Webster, Billy Harrison, Jack Jolly, Leonard Abbot, unknown, unknown, Ted Horsepool

Second row (left to right): Ted Pearson, unknown, Maud Leeland, Mary Titman, Mr Levack, Elsie Godby, unknown, David Harrison, Leonard Pearson

Third row (left to right): Billy Vergette, Elsie Titman, Mabel Saunders, unknown, Phyllis Pearson, Connie Potter, Nellie Smith, unknown, Betty Adams, Alf Wilkinson

Back row (left to right): Jessie Saunders, Gertie Horsepool, unknown, Sewell, Kathleen Pearson, Ida Smith, Freda Thornton

Mrs E. Gale of Glinton has named the majority; does anyone remember the missing names?

PEAKIRK, c. 1910

The small village of Peakirk lies about seven miles north-west of Peterborough. This monument, known locally as the "Cross", was erected in 1904 by Canon Edward James, a past rector, who came to Peakirk as a curate and completed nearly sixty years service here. This card, incorrectly captioned 'The Green', shows the house on the left, which is now divided into two dwellings, and the large house in the centre, which has been demolished to make room for road widening. Peakirk is notable for the Wildfowl Trust reserve founded by Sir Peter Scott.

RECTORY RD PEAKIRK.

PEAKIRK, p.u. 1910

In this desolate swamp, more than 1200 years ago, St Pega, sister of St Guthlac, founded for herself a little hermitage. A Christian church, the only one dedicated to St Pega, has stood here ever since. The large house in the centre of the photograph is ''The Chestnuts'', but it was never the rectory as the caption on the card indicates. Now called Chestnut Close, the cottages on the left are no longer there.

PEAKIRK, 1960s

Over the south door of St Pega's church there is "an 800 year-old masterpiece of carving in its tympanum" — TYMPANUM is the stonework that fills the space within the top of an arch. "At the base is a group of fan-shaped designs, and the arch expands with seven bands of carvings, all different, probably 200 pieces of ornament so clear and well-preserved that it seems incredible it has been here all these centuries. The other Norman doorway at the north entrance is a plain round arch cut from a single stone". Within the church are a series of medieval wall-paintings, which date from the fourteenth century and were discovered in 1949. There is a separate guide to these in the church by F. Clive Rouse.

PEAKIRK, 1912

In July/August 1912, the Boat Inn almost lived up to its name when the River Welland and the Roman-built Car Dyke burst their banks and flooded the main B1443 from Peakirk to Newborough. The gates of the aptly-named Folly Crossing, on the GNR loop line to Grimsby, can be seen in the distance. The figure in the doorway of the Boat could be that of Mr J. Dudley, who was proprietor in 1912, and continued until replaced in 1927 by Mr W. Jones. The inn finally closed in the early 1930s and became a private house. Behind the premises to the left of this picture was an old osier bed through which passed Car Dyke. This is now the home of the **Peakirk Wildfowl Trust.**

NEWBOROUGH, 1893

Halfway between Peakirk and Newborough is the Duck Decoy, held by the Williams family until 1958, and now managed by the Wild Fowl Trust. In 1670 the Decoyman (Mr Williams) was granted permission to pierce the River Welland to lead water to his Decoy Pond. The area of water in the pond is 2½ acres, set within enclosed woodland covering 18 to 19 acres. The pond or pool is octagonal and has eight 'pipes' or channels leading towards the 8 main points of the compass. Each pipe is netted over from end to end and the prevailing wind direction determines which pipe is used for decoying the ducks, using Piper, a dog trained for this purpose. Years ago ducks were caught and killed for the eating tables of the gentry in the towns — now they are caught and ringed by the Wild Fowl Trust and then released to fly again. The Newborough Decoy is the oldest of the few surviving decoys.

NEWBOROUGH, p.u. 1908

Borough Fen was originally 3000 acres of waste and commonland in the Nassaburgh Hundred, and belonged to the Abbey of Peterborough. In 1819 the first common was enclosed, causing upheaval with the local people. Newborough Parish was formed in 1823 from the Old Borough. In 1830, the church, dedicated to St Bartholomew, was erected and gradually a new community was created around the Church. In 1848 a vicarage was built, in 1852 a school and a Methodist Chapel in the 1860s. In 1911 the population of Newborough was 723. On the east side of Newborough Church is rich fen land reputed to "grow the best spuds ever". The sole message on the reverse of this postcard reads: "Oh! The Wind!" aptly commenting on the east wind which sweeps straight off the sea across the flat fens with no shelter from its icy blast.

Gunton's Road, Newborough.

NEWBOROUGH, 1930s

This is the main road into Newborough from Dogsthorpe (formerly Dodsthorpe), Peterborough. It is said to be named after Symon Gunton, Vicar of St John's, Peterborough, 1660-1666, a Prebendary of the Church of Peterburgh and co-author of "The History of the Church of Peterburgh", although on old maps it seems to be listed as White Post Road. This main road through the fens to Crowland intersects with the B1443 Peakirk to Thorney road at Bull Bridge, where The Bull public house was once a stopping place for coaches. After crossing the B1443, the Crowland road once continued through Willow Drove (formerly High Drove) to High Bank and Crowland, past Eardley Grange, home of Lord Eardley, who once owned Borough Fen.

NEWBOROUGH, c. 1912

Norwood Farm was once called Norwood House and was home to a distillery making peppermint oil. Situated on Guntons Road, it was the home of the Bellairs family and Mr C Bellairs, born in 1908, remembers the distillery being in a state of disrepair when he was a young boy. This was mainly due to the fact that the Germans had undercut the price of peppermint oil, putting the distillery out of business. Peppermint water was a popular remedy for colds and stomach disorders.

Eye Village, near Peterborough
T. W. R. Series

EYE, c. 1906

The empty village street is in marked contrast to the A47 of today, with its heavy traffic en route for the east coast. The completion of a new bypass will perhaps bring peace to the village once more. In the distance can be seen the church of St Matthew, built in 1846, and the broach spire which was dismantled in 1982 when found to be unsafe. The terraced houses in the right foreground still front the Peterborough road today.

EYE GREEN, c. 1921

Nothing much remains of this scene near the Crowland Road bridge at Eye Green. The Midland and Great Northern Joint railway station was officially opened on the 1 August 1886, with Isaac Hallam as stationmaster. Nine years later there were seven trains a day into Peterborough and six in the opposite direction. The last freight train (carrying bricks) left the station on the 16 April 1966. The Northam brickyard started working in 1897 and in the following year brickyard labourers earned 4½d per hour for a 56½-hour week. The brickyard chimneys were finally demolished in December 1990.

FLAG FEN

Flag Fen, or Peterborough Common, named after the irises that grew there, had an exclusive right to stock forty-eight sheep on its land, from Lady Day to Martinmas every year. In the Enclosure Act of 1811 this is attested by seven butchers of Peterborough. The Peterborough race meetings were also held at Flag Fen, but now it is more well known as one of the best-preserved Bronze Age sites in Europe. This listed building known as Flag Fen House is of eighteenth century origin and is situated between Newark Road and Edgerley Drain Road.

WOODSTON, c. 1911

The Soke of Peterborough extended the length of the Oundle Road to its junction with New Road. Looking north towards Peterborough this view shows, on the corner of Jubilee Street, the butcher's shop of Huntings, who were trading here as far back as the 1890s. It can be noted that the butcher's cart has all the meat loose in the back; no pre-wrapped meat in those days! In the middle of the picture, in the distance, is the former site of the first Baptist chapel erected in Woodston at a cost of £500. A supermarket now occupies the site.

WOODSTON, c. 1904

About half a mile from the city centre on the southern side of the River Nene is Woodston. The handbill on the wall spells it Woodstone, and advertises for sale by local firm Fox and Vergette, cottages and a butcher's shop. The sale was held in March 1904 at the Angel Hotel in Peterborough. This terraced house at 130 Palmerston Road is still there today, minus the iron railings. At the door stands a former occupant, Mrs Hardiment, with her daughter Hetty and a young neighbour.

FLETTON AVENUE.

FLETTON, p.u. 1905

Returning from Whittlesey to Peterborough, along Fletton Avenue, opposite Fairfield Road, the traveller had a clear view of The Peacock public house on London Road, with the Mill behind it. The gateway and part of the railings on the left remain and would seem to be the entrance to Fletton Spring, which rose somewhere here and crossed Fletton Avenue to come out on the opposite side of Spring Fields. This Spring forms the southern boundary of the Soke of Peterborough. In 1905 solid villas were built here in this very pleasant tree-lined avenue, with seats for the weary to rest awhile.

FLETTON, c. 1912

Rightly called the home of the brick-making industry, Fletton's London Brick Co. had the largest kiln in the world in the 1920s, the old B1 off Fletton High Street. This large house situated on the corner of Fletton Avenue and Fletton High Street has been replaced by a one-storey hairdressing salon. The parish church of St Margaret can just be seen behind the trees and Church Lane, to the left of the picture, still exists today.

FLETTON, 1930s

This lovely church in Fletton Avenue, dedicated to St Margaret, has the very finest examples of Anglo-Saxon carvings dating from the eighth or ninth centuries, set below the chancel east window behind the altar; and two early twelfth-century stone panels, carved with figures of an angel and a saint under round arches, were set into the south wall of the chancel in 1901. These are believed to be Norman. In the churchyard is a twelfth-century Anglo-Saxon cross which once had the familiar "Celtic" type wheelhead, unfortunately now broken. Rich carvings once adorned the much-weathered shaft. The church is built of Barnack stone, with a fine broach spire. Later in the 1880s, in the village of Fletton, a unique British industry developed — the brick industry, made possible by the Hempsted brothers' discovery of the properties of the Lower Oxford Clay — "The Clay That Burns".

STANGROUND, c. 1905

Beyond this building, with its imposing Tuscan columns, can be seen the spire of St John the Baptist's church, built in the early fourteenth century. Situated at the corner of Church Street and Copper Beech Way, this was the old vicarage, and one of its former occupants, from 1905-1916, was the Rev. E.G. Swain, a well-known writer of ghost stories. Today, in complete contrast, it houses the city's Polish Ex-Servicemen's Club.

PETERBOROUGH MAGISTRATES COURT

The Courts of Petty Sessions were held in the Sessions House, Thorpe Road, from 1844 for over 130 years, until the new Magistrates Court in Lower Bridge Street was opened by Her Majesty the Queen on the 22 March 1978. The Crown Court also moved here temporarily in August 1980 until 1987 when it moved to its new premises in Bishop's Road. A plaque inside reads: "For centuries past justice around Peterborough was administered from Langdyke Bush, near Castor Hanglands... The old Double Hundred Court of Nassaburgh which controlled Burgh (Peterborough) and District".

(Photograph by Reg Wilcox, Minster Photographic, 1991)

PETERBOROUGH CROWN COURT & COUNTY COURT

The Crown Court moved from its temporary site within the new Magistrates Court in Lower Bridge Street, and the County Court moved from its former premises in New Road, on the corner of Cattle Market Road, to these premises which were officially opened by HRH The Duke of Gloucester GCVO on Friday 15 May 1987. The site of this new Combined Court was many years ago within the grounds of the Bishop's Palace. Thus a link with the extraordinary privileges of the past is retained.

(Photograph by Reg Wilcox, Minster Photographic, 1991)

PETERBOROUGH COUNTY COURT, 1989

Until the passing of the County Courts Act in 1846 the Bailiff of the Dean and Chapter held a Civil Court in the chamber above the Minster Gateway, known as the Court of Common Pleas. The newly-established County Court was held monthly in the Sessions House, Thorpe Road, and the Registrar's Office was in the Cathedral Gateway. In 1873 this building was erected by H.M. Commissioner of Works in New Road, on the corner of Cattle Market Road (now Laxton Square) and all County Court business transferred there, together with the District Probate Registry. This continued in use until December 1986 when the County Court transferred to the Combined Crown Court and County Court in Bishop's Road, Peterborough. These premises are now occupied by Rinaldo's Club.

(Photograph by Peter E. Harvey, Secretary of Peterborough Photographic Society, 1989)

DOGSTHORPE, c. 1908

This rather neglected-looking old house stood on the site of a modern housing development called Dovecote Close, off the Welland Road. One of the last surviving late-seventeenth-century/early eighteenth-century houses in this part of Dogsthorpe, this was probably quite a grand building in its time. Nevertheless the family standing outside, with the girls looking smart in their clean white pinafores, are in complete contrast to their surroundings.

DOGSTHORPE, c. 1929

This photograph was taken by Mr J. Searle of Werrington and shows preparations for the laying of the sewer along Dogsthorpe Road, just before its junction with St Paul's Road. The Bluebell public house is in the background on the right-hand side; with a glimpse of the Holman Generator which powered the drills. The motor bike is a Triumph, registration ER 4004, and provided independent transport for its proud owner. Others less fortunate perhaps caught a tram at the nearby terminus; two tram poles are evident on the right of the photograph.

PASTON VALLEY, p.u. 1913

This lovely "tree-studded resort" was given to Peterborough Corporation as a gift; and later the area of about three acres beyond the fence on the left was laid out as a pleasure ground, before being handed over to the Corporation as Itter Memorial Park, in memory of Arthur Itter, Mayor of Peterborough in 1934 for six short weeks prior to his sudden death. The message on the postcard reads: "I hope you will like this postcard, but I needn't ask you that, because you have sat many a time behind these tree trunks in the dark have you not dear that's how he talks to you isn't it A?"

PASTON, p.u. 1911

A view of All Saint's Church at Paston, from Fulbridge Road at its junction with Hallfields Lane and Paston Lane. The grassy triangles in the road are now replaced by a large roundabout, with colourful flower beds throughout the year. It is very difficult to imagine this as "the Church in the Fields" with a delightful view across green meadows to the hamlets of Gunthorpe, Walton and Werrington (which were all originally within the Parish of Paston) as the church is now surrounded by housing estates and has been absorbed into Peterborough. However, there are still some trees left within the churchyard, to remind us of its former identity, and the avenue of limes still leads to the south door — a handsome lych-gate has been erected over this western entrance.

PASTON, 1922

Bishop Wood, Reverend Donaldson and Brigadier General W. Strong, CB, CMG, JP, officiate at the Dedication Ceremony on 17 September 1922, of the Lych Gate, erected in memory of those who fell in the Great War. Each side of the gate bears the inscription ''The Gateway of Remembrance''. Later, further names were added in memory of those who died in the Second World War.

PASTON

Local residents would not recognise this quiet tree-lined lane, once the local venue for cycle rides and leisurely walks. Now known as Hallfields Lane, it leads to the modern housing estate at Paston. Taking its name from Hall Field, owned in 1805 by William Morland, the field was actually situated at the other side of the Fulbridge Road. In the background can be seen parts of the walls and outbuildings of Paston Hall, demolished in 1958 and last occupied by Mr F.C. Ihlee.

GUNTHORPE, early 1900s

Mrs Clara Hadman, wife of Mr Robert H. Hadman, stands with one of her children outside the farm at Gunthorpe Road. This fine old stone house had been in the family since the late 1800s and was demolished in 1958 to make way for the new housing estates spreading northwards from the City of Peterborough. When her father-in-law, Mr Henry Hadman, went to live at Gunthorpe, it was remote from Peterborough, surrounded by green fields. From 1895 to 1908 the house was in the occupation of Mr R.H. Hadman, from 1908 to 1936 Mrs C. Hadman and since 1936 Mr and Mrs R.H.J. Hadman, who remained there until it was demolished. Their dairy farm was well known to local residents, and later they specialised in pigs and poultry. The double-fronted house was solidly built of Barnack stone, with two massive stone buttresses apparently built at the same time as the house.

COW SHED. GUNTHORPE DAIRY FARM.

GUNTHORPE, c. 1930

Not many photographs were taken of the small hamlet of Gunthorpe, so this one of the dairy farm at Gunthorpe Grange is quite unusual. Standing opposite Hadman's Dairy Farm, both houses were originally part of the Paston Hall Estate when Mr Fred Pratt lived at Paston Hall and farmed the whole of Paston and Gunthorpe. Local legend has it that Mr Pratt used Gunthorpe Grange as a store for bone-meal fertiliser. It is said that the bones were crushed in the drawing room, with the engine on the lawn and a belt passing through the window!

WALTON, c. 1960

This aerial view was taken before the Rhubarb road bridge over the Lincoln Road was demolished in October 1961 and replaced in 1971 by the Soke Parkway flyover. The railway bridge over the main line was demolished a little later in December 1961. In the foreground can be seen the Railway Sports ground and the fields on the left have been replaced by the Bretton township. Beyond the bridge can be seen the C.W.S. Wagon Works, the maltings of Gilstrap, Earp & Co. and the extensive works of Peter Brotherhood. Most of this latter area has been replaced by a large shopping complex.

WALTON, 1945

Everyone is enjoying themselves at this giant street party to celebrate VE Day. Taken from the upstairs of Sharps general store (now International Boys' Town Shop) the festive tables were erected at the junction of Willesden Avenue and Churchfield Road. Mothers baked cakes and fathers worked hard to make it a memorable day for the children from all the surrounding streets. Similar celebrations took place all over the country.

WALTON, c. 1920

This group picture, including four employees holding guns, was taken outside the front doors of the engineering firm of Peter Brotherhood Ltd at Walton. Sitting directly behind the silver cups is Peter Brotherhood's successor, his son Stanley. In 1906 the company moved from its London factory to Peterborough, where in 1907 the first Brotherhood's Steam Turbine was designed and manufactured. The first sports club opened on land in Marholm Road in 1908 with twenty members. After a short period on a playing field behind the Paul Pry Inn, the club obtained a new site in 1918 in Occupation Road, New England.

WALTON

In order to avoid crossing the lines of the Midland Railway System, the originally planned route of the Great Northern Railway was changed to run parallel to MRS lines as far as Helpston. The double level crossing at Walton is shown here with the station, which closed on 7 December 1953. On the afternoon of 28 March 1916, in one of the worst storms in living memory, a goods train on the stretch between Walton and Werrington became entangled when telegraph poles and wires collapsed on top of it.

WERRINGTON, 1910

Werrington has always enjoyed its village celebrations, and the accession of George V on 6 May 1910 was no exception. The picture shows the village green, then called Pond Street, and the Methodist Chapel (Wesleyan), built in 1835, to the left. In the centre is Thorney Lodge, dating from pre-1766 and sold in 1910 for £200. Now a very attractive family dwelling, it was then occupied by Messrs Cole and Stimson in the front and Messrs Trowell and Eyett in two cottages at the back.

HALL LANE, WERRINGTON.

WERRINGTON, c. 1920

At the west end of The Green, at its junction with Church Street, stands the village shop, owned by Mr J.W. Searle, grocer and draper; within its old stone walls lay a cornucopia of goods to suit every whim. On a triangle of grass in front of the house on the corner stood one of the very few village street lamps. Evenings with a full moon must have been eagerly awaited! The road on the left is Hall Lane, leading to Foxcovert Road (to Glinton and Peakirk), and Fenbridge Road (to Newborough).

WERRINGTON, c. 1920

This Ford van stands outside Searle's Shop on The Green. Research has, as yet, revealed nothing on "Olympia Agricultural Company Limited", but this may have been one of the co-operative concerns formed after the First World War to help returning soldiers to run smallholdings successfully. This photograph may have been taken by John Searle, son of Mr J.W. Searle who owned the shop in the background. He was one of the village photographers and gave slide shows in the shop in the evenings, still remembered by some of Werrington's oldest residents. Many local postcards are evidence of his photographic prowess.